Self-Esteem

A Comprehensive Manual Offering Expert Advice On Effectively Confronting Personal Fears And Cultivating Unwavering Self Confidence

(Expand Your Horizons And Venture Beyond The Confines Of Familiarity)

Oswaldo Jacobs

TABLE OF CONTENT

How To Assume The Protagonist Role In Your Personal Journey 1

Indications That One Is Evading Accountability For Their Self-Esteem... 51

Attaining Cognitive Lucidity: Recommended Actions And Destinations... 63

The Profound Influence Of Self-Assurance 84

Suggestions To Enhance Motivation 117

How To Assume The Protagonist Role In Your Personal Journey

Many individuals navigate through existence without establishing commendable personal benchmarks. They become relegated to the role of a minor character in the narrative of their own existence, despite their rightful entitlement to possess qualities of equal distinction, courage, admiration, and intelligence as the protagonist. Although it is a universally accepted truth that real life does not mirror the unrealistic portrayals seen in movies, it should not discourage you from assuming the role of the hero who comes to the rescue.

What strategies can one employ to cultivate the self-assurance needed to assume the role of protagonist in one's own personal narrative? The following instructions outline the actions you are required to take:

First and foremost, make the conscious decision to pursue improvement. You hold the ultimate authority over your own life, independent of the influence exerted by your family, friends, or employer.

Be aware that in this realm, you shall find yourself as your unwavering ally. Although it is undeniable that your relationships hold significance, it is important to acknowledge that your thoughts, behaviors, and choices ultimately determine your circumstance. Once you make the conscious choice to assume responsibility for your own actions, a notable shift in your perspective will become apparent.

Proceed to articulate with utmost clarity the specific objectives you aspire to accomplish in your lifetime.

Articulate your intended objective, regardless of its nature, audibly to yourself. You are affirming to yourself and the cosmic order that you are embarking upon a transformative odyssey towards a desired objective.

This objective will instill within you a sense of having led a remarkable existence on this mortal plane.

Step 3: Proceed with the necessary course of action!

Equip yourself with a well-defined strategy and leverage the resources at your disposal. Acquire knowledge from daily experiences, always bearing in mind that errors and setbacks serve as invaluable instructors. Appreciate and cultivate valuable friendships. Acquire knowledge and understanding from your mentors. Above all, it is crucial not to underestimate the value of the current moment as once it elapses, time cannot be reclaimed.

Acquire a clear understanding of your desires and assume the role of the mastermind behind your journey towards attaining your objectives.

Devote a portion of each day to cultivating self-motivation and maintaining a steadfast course. Primarily, ensure to derive enjoyment from the experience. By prioritizing and actively pursuing the core values that resonate with you in life, a sense of confidence will swiftly ensue.

Gaining Confidence

One challenge that individuals grappling with self-esteem difficulties encounter is their tendency to magnify circumstances. They engage in this behavior unwittingly; however, it is simply their approach to coping with existence. For instance, please elaborate on the potential consequences that could arise from an error in your actions. One may perceive it as a form of humiliation and confirmation of one's inadequacy. Such a characterization is completely unfounded, and it appears to stem from a personal issue regarding your self-worth. The shortcomings witnessed today often transform into subjects of amusement in the future.

If one perceives themselves to be unsuccessful in an endeavor, they should commence by gradually taking small measures towards developing self-assurance. To attain confidence, it is imperative to ensure that one is given ample opportunity to engage in activities at which they possess proficiency. Each individual possesses inherent strengths, and even individuals who struggle with self-esteem and confidence will demonstrate areas of exceptional ability. To ascertain the nature of these occupations, we recommend adopting a proactive approach wherein you allocate a dedicated period to situate yourself, armed with a blank sheet of paper, and meticulously document the activities that genuinely engross and captivate you. Typically, individuals derive pleasure from engaging in activities that fall within their realm of familiarity. To provide an illustration, I derive great pleasure from the practice of culinary arts and possess a discernible level of proficiency in this domain. Although your preferences may vary, these suggestions serve as commendable foundations to cultivate self-assurance.

Your daily routine ought to encompass a proportionate allocation of activities in which you demonstrate proficiency, as such engagements aid in the cultivation of self-assurance. The rationale behind its effectiveness lies in the fact that engaging in activities within one's comfort zone for half of the time equates to a 50 percent increment in positive reinforcement for self-assurance. Ensure that you select activities that you find enjoyable and that seamlessly align with your daily routines.

I can attest that during the initial phase of my engagement with the publisher as an article writer, I experienced extreme distress, manifesting in psychological and physiological manifestations such as increased frustration, vocal expression of distress, and heightened anxiety, which persisted for the duration of the first week. The task was exceedingly challenging, requiring the production of a substantial amount of content within a limited timeframe. My aptitude for time management was lacking. Although I possessed some familiarity with the subject matter I was writing about, my knowledge base was not substantial enough to efficiently meet the time constraints. Throughout my early childhood, an aversion to impending deadlines became ingrained in me, prompting me to go to great lengths to evade them. Regrettably, this detrimental habit had adverse effects on both my academic performance during college and my professional standing in subsequent employments. I derived personal satisfaction from the autonomy afforded by the occupation outlined in the article, as it enabled me to establish my own timetable and exercise a certain level of discretion in selecting subject matter for composition. Nonetheless, amidst such considerable stress, I perceived a lack of proficiency in my abilities and, occasionally, had the inclination to relinquish my efforts and resign due to a pervasive fear of failure and mounting frustration.

I derive great pleasure from the act of writing; I found immense gratification in the opportunities that the job presented for fostering a successful vocation as a writer, coupled with the liberties it afforded me. Therefore, rather than forsaking one of my passions due to succumbing to the apprehension of failure and the overwhelming sense of self-defeat that was eroding my self-assurance, I resolved to persevere. I came to the realization that a shift in my perspective regarding deadlines and my work methodology was necessary. The pivotal moment occurred when I assumed the responsibility of extensively studying the enterprise in which I was on the verge of participating. I extensively researched accomplished writers and actively sought out the advice they shared. I commenced documenting the instances during which I engaged in work, as well as the intervals in which I took breaks or experienced distractions, with the purpose of aiding my efforts in maintaining productivity, enhancing concentration, and fostering a sense of regularity. Regarding article topics about which I lacked sufficient knowledge, I allocated a significant amount of time in advance to conduct extensive research, ensuring that when the time to write arrived, the information would be recent and presented in a coherent manner.

All of these factors proved beneficial in enabling me to acquire greater impetus in my practice. I experienced a restoration in my self-assurance, providing a sense of comfort. Nevertheless, I observed that I continued to fall below the desired standard in meeting those challenging deadlines. Despite making progress in enhancing my work efficiency, I experienced persistent stress merely from the concept of working under time constraints. Consequently, in this state of anxiety, I consistently succumbed to procrastination instead of fulfilling my responsibilities. During my time at the workplace, I experienced a gradual onset of contemplation regarding the subject matter of the article, accompanied by an inherent hinderance in mental clarity attributable to the burden of stress. The latent recollections of previous academic and occupational disappointments were subtly impeding my professional performance. My self-confidence was further diminished, leading to the resurgence of self-doubt.

They hold grudges.

Joel and Diana were joined in matrimony for a duration of 7 years. They possess an idyllic union. They are the parents of two children and their affection for one another is apparent. They appear to possess all the necessary attributes.

At some point, Diana engaged in conversation with Joel. She expressed to him her present dissatisfaction with their marital relationship, and disclosed that she has been engaging in a romantic involvement with her superior at work over the course of the past two months.

Joel was beyond devastated. He began instigating conflict on social media and ensured that his acquaintances were informed of Diana's extramarital involvement.

Nevertheless, even after the passage of 2 years, Joel's bitterness remains unchanged, mirroring his emotional state when Diana shattered his heart. He has become toxic. He consistently exhibits anger and persistently engages in defamation towards the mother of his children whenever possible. He is unable to simply release everything.

Toxic people hold grudges. They raise attention to your previous errors with the intention of generating conflict. They are unable to progress or let go. They emanate an adverse energy that induces sensations of physical weakness and dizziness.

They fail to assume accountability for their actions.

They consistently deflect responsibility for any wrongdoing. They attribute their difficulties to the actions of others. They fail to assume accountability for their actions and the course of their lives.

They are inconsistent.

It seems as though they exhibit symptoms akin to dissociative identity disorder. They adapt their demeanor, conduct, and character to exert influence over others and obtain their desires.

They possess a chilling demeanor akin to the icy touch of winter.

They are not supportive. They employ love deprivation as a means of exerting control and coercing compliance with their desires.

They lack empathy.

An aptitude for empathy serves as a robust indicator of a sound and balanced personality. Individuals displaying vampiric energy tendencies frequently lack profound empathy. They encounter difficulty comprehending the experiences and perspectives of others.

They possess an inflated sense of self-importance.

Toxic individuals frequently manifest an exaggerated sense of self-worth. They possess a sense of intellectual superiority and perceive themselves as superior to those in their vicinity. They possess a sense of omniscience.

They are abusive.

Certain individuals exhibiting toxic behavior can be categorized as inherently malevolent. They possess the capacity to engage in both physical and emotional mistreatment. They would engage in actions that bring disgrace and abuse upon you. They would exert pressure upon you to relinquish your authority, thereby enabling them to pursue their own agenda.

Diverse Classifications of Energy Drainers

Empaths typically attract energy vampires due to their innate qualities of kindness and empathy. They frequently indulge in the consumption of empaths' energy.

If you happen to identify as an empath or possess a heightened sensitivity, it would be advisable for you to distance yourself from the subsequent individuals who drain your energy.

Drama Queen

Ara has achieved great success in the realm of film production. She possesses great intellectual capacity and exhibits exceptional aptitude in the field of writing. She possesses an acute sense of humor and an enchanting physical allure. Nevertheless, she consistently desires attention and partakes in behavior aimed at garnering it. She possesses a pronounced inclination towards entitlement.

She consistently provokes dramatic circumstances. She will exert influence over others through manipulation. Her penchant for fabricating rumors with the sole intention of inciting conflicts is apparent. She derives pleasure from instigating conflicts among her friends solely for her amusement. Furthermore, she exhibits an unwavering fixation on attaining an impeccable physical appearance and embodying flawlessness. She becomes extremely agitated or overly emotional over minor matters.

Drama queens lack any sense of personal responsibility for their actions and the course of their lives. They initiate rumors with the intention of generating theatricality and discord. They derive pleasure from instigating conflict among individuals. They frequently employ henchmen to assist in dismantling their adversaries.

These individuals exhibit not only toxic behavior. They are also shallow. They exhibit a heightened sense of cataclysmic anticipation solely due to the negative circumstances they are currently experiencing. They derive pleasure from being the focal point of attention.

Jealous Jane

Marie enjoys a high quality of life. She is a resident of the United States who currently resides on the picturesque island of Capri. All aspects of his life appear to be in a state of perfection.

Nevertheless, upon accessing her Instagram account, she observes her acquaintances joyously reveling in luxurious destinations such as Bali and Maldives. Upon viewing the wedding photos of her friends, she experienced a profound sense of being absent from life's myriad opportunities.

She consistently demonstrates a state of discontentment and voices grievances concerning even the most minor matters. She fails to acknowledge the full value of her possessions.

Individuals who experience envy possess a potent, detrimental energy that poses significant risks to those with empathic abilities. These individuals exhibit diminished levels of self-assurance. They are emotionally unstable. They criticize and belittle others as a means to mask their own inner insecurities.

Temperamental Tom

Albert is generally exemplary in his conduct. He possesses a disposition marked by benevolence and magnanimity. Nevertheless, he exhibits a propensity for anger. He experiences heightened emotional reactions to minor incidents and struggles to effectively manage his anger.

In moments of anger, he tends to hurl any object within his reach. He consistently exploits those in his vicinity to serve as receptacles for his emotional turmoil. He frequently shares his emotional burdens at every available opportunity.

Erratic individuals can be both mentally exhausting and intimidating. Frequent contact with these individuals of a deleterious nature has the potential to result in severe psychological distress.

Manipulating Mark

Manipulative individuals are cunning and deceitful in their actions, often masquerading as your confidant. They will dedicate time to familiarize themselves with the factors that can bring you happiness. They will utilize this information with the intention of coercing you into acquiescing to their desires.

These individuals frequently adopt the role of the victim. They would embellish their personal concerns in an effort to elicit your sympathy. They employ a strategic means of deception by selectively revealing only partial truths in order to achieve their desired objectives.

Frequently, they will exert pressure upon you or resort to passive aggressive actions in order to compel you to adopt their perspective.

Arrogant Arman

Individuals with an inflated sense of self-regard perceive every situation as a contest. They hold the conviction that they possess a greater level of superiority compared to their peers, displaying occasional tendencies towards arrogance.

These individuals engage in the amplification of their capabilities with the intent of instilling a sense of inadequacy within oneself. They consistently boast about their achievements. They frequently exhibit discourteous and unkind behavior.

Interacting with individuals who display a strong sense of superiority can be exceptionally exhausting, especially for individuals who possess a high degree of empathy.

Blaming Bens

Attributing Ben's tendency to play the victim. They have a proclivity for attributing all of their hardships to external individuals. They fail to assume accountability for their actions or their overall life circumstances.

Selfish Sam

Selfish individuals are those who place a higher priority on their personal self-interest. These individuals possess a slight inclination towards narcissism. They will exert all efforts to obtain their desired outcome.

The Critic

We can all benefit from receiving constructive feedback on occasion. Nevertheless, the Critic fails to provide additional feedback to bolster their development. Their main objective is to dismantle others in order to derive a sense of personal satisfaction.

Let us consider Gina as an illustrative case. She previously held the title of a beauty queen, however, her physical appearance has noticeably diminished. This elicited feelings of resentment and ire in her.

Her acrimony compelled her to pass judgment on those in her vicinity. Despite weighing only 125 pounds, she would make it a point to inform her daughter of her weight concerns. On a daily basis, she would offer critiques and feedback to her staff. She utilizes derogatory remarks to bolster her own self-esteem and enhance her perception of her own personal circumstances.

The Queen of Ice

Having a strong sense of empathy is a crucial characteristic as it enables one to gain a comprehensive understanding of individuals in their vicinity. It facilitates the ability to empathetically immerse oneself in the perspective of others and gain a genuine understanding of their everyday experiences. It facilitates the formation of remarkable interpersonal connections.

Ice queens are individuals who exhibit a distinct lack of empathy and compassion. They exhibit a lack of respect, dis interest, and an unresponsiveness They instill within you a sense of inadequacy, disregarding your emotional distress, hardships, and even your essential requirements.

It commences with a shift in perspective. Consider introspectively and reflect upon your own qualities, what aspects of myself should I critique? For what reason do I engage in self-criticism? Initially, it is crucial to discern the manner in which you undermine your own confidence. This process may be comparatively less challenging for certain individuals. Certain individuals experience concerns regarding their physical appearance. Individuals who exhibit a strong aversion to their physical appearance, or engage in self-critical behavior and may even extend this negativity towards others due to their appearance, are experiencing a condition referred to as body dysmorphic disorder. This individual will be required to acquire the proficiency in performing two tasks. The initial step is to determine their desired course of action and assess their actual capacity for making changes to their appearance. This could be regarded as an initiation of engaging in jogging or any alternative form of physical activity. It may entail adopting a healthier dietary regimen. Regardless of the outcome, it is imperative that the chosen course of action remains both accessible and mild. The subsequent undertaking entails relinquishing any negative thoughts or perceptions regarding your physical appearance. One may choose to disregard that notion and instead state,

"I have been engaging in regular exercise, a measure I can undertake to enhance my physical appearance." That will suffice in terms of the tasks I need to address in this particular field. Please disregard the remaining tasks. One must confront the inner voice that asserts one's appearance as dreadful and repulsive, recognizing that this voice essentially emanates from within oneself. Occasionally, individuals of a bullying or abusive nature manifest in our existence, who proceed to relay derogatory remarks to us about our own selves. Frequently, however, it originates from the depths of our own consciousness.

Positive thinking entails adopting a mindset that transcends pessimism and desolation, instead recognizing and appreciating the frequent encounters with beauty in one's life. There exist beautiful experiences in our lives; however, we often fail to grasp the experiences that are readily available to us. Positive thinking encompasses a slight shift in perspective, transitioning from a negative mindset such as "I dislike the darkness outside and have no desire to go to work" to a more positive outlook such as "Though it is dark outside, I will exert my best efforts at work and perhaps indulge in a brief rest afterwards." This perspective acknowledges that life is not always filled with ideal circumstances. Positive thinking should align with practicality and achievability.

Addressing motivation is of utmost significance, particularly within individuals suffering from depression. Motivation plays a crucial role in the development and manifestation of depression. The absence of motivation is the underlying factor behind depression, and frequently, this gives rise to a cycle wherein the absence of motivation and negative emotions reinforce one another. Motivation is an abstract notion, yet it can be asserted with considerable certainty that enhanced physical well-being tends to engender heightened levels of motivation. By devoting all your time to addiction or engaging in unhealthy habits, you are perpetuating this cycle and undermining your motivation. This is regrettable, yet it is not uncommon.

A significant aspect of cultivating a positive mindset involves the acquisition of skills to engage self-dialogue that focuses on positive aspects of life, whilst simultaneously detaching oneself from negative thoughts. One can simply acknowledge that thoughts hold no factual basis. There is no obligation for you to actively refute or invalidate your thoughts; alternatively, you may simply acknowledge them as unkind or unnecessary, permitting you to discard them subsequently. Many individuals highly prioritize their thoughts, these minute cognitive expressions, and their respective contents. Subsequently, they allocate their time exclusively to strategic contemplation in an effort to attain a sense of fulfillment. However, the sense of fulfillment remains elusive.

It would be beneficial in this situation to acquire the ability to articulate your statements effectively. One's thoughts do not define their identity. Your thoughts are solely confined to the realm of your mind. Occasionally, their assertions or claims are accurate and valid, while at other times, they are not. It does not matter. Regardless of the circumstance, they do not constitute your identity. Your character is not inherently virtuous or morally flawed based on your thoughts or beliefs.

Ideas spontaneously emerge in the mind, as they are not consciously produced. Ideas represent a highly conceptual flow of consciousness that manifests itself in the form of language or imagery. They are not real. However, you possess the capability to manifest them. As an illustration, suppose you contemplate the idea of strolling outside in the sunlight tomorrow, and subsequently proceed to actually take a walk outdoors on said day. In this scenario, you have conceived of a notion and subsequently transformed it into tangible reality.

Nevertheless, it did not attain reality until you executed it. Ideas cannot be readily accessed by outside individuals, as they reside exclusively within the confines of one's private cognitive realm. Now, it is essential that you attend to the maintenance of that particular area, exercising discretion in determining which elements should be included and which should be excluded. This platform offers you the opportunity to cultivate a continuous flow of fresh and optimistic ideas pertaining to both yourself and the world. Commence developing thoughts that will facilitate your progress towards reaching your full potential. Commence the practice of acknowledging and celebrating your acts of kindness towards yourself and others. Self-care is extremely important.

Developing a positive mindset cannot be acquired instantaneously. However, by cultivating a mindset of self-compassion and refraining from passing judgment upon oneself, it is possible to initiate a transformation in one's cognition. You shall discover an enhanced capacity for compassion, heightened wisdom, and a fortified spirit.

Optimism

In the upcoming chapter, our focus will be directed towards an exploration of optimism and its impact on one's life. However, prior to delving into the subject matter, it is essential to establish a fundamental understanding of optimism in its most rudimentary guise.

What Is Optimism

Optimism can be defined as the state of possessing confidence and a hopeful attitude when it comes to future outcomes and the broader concept of the future. It entails a sense of assurance regarding successful outcomes. Positivity is a characteristic that an individual can embody. It can be stated that an individual harbors a sense of optimism, or that they "possess a disposition of optimism." Optimism can be directed towards a specific matter, or it may prevail as a general characteristic of their personality. An individual can adopt a positive outlook towards the future, harbor optimism concerning the resolution of a particular issue or occurrence, or embody an optimistic disposition. Optimism encompasses an individual's perspective or outlook on the future of a particular entity or the future in a broader sense. It bears resemblance to optimism or adopting a positive outlook, however, it encompasses a stronger conviction. Individuals with an optimistic disposition demonstrate a proclivity for directing their attention towards favorable aspects, as opposed to fixating on adverse ones.

Strategies for Developing a Positive Outlook

Not everybody possesses an innate disposition towards optimism, however, the acquisition of this mindset is attainable for anyone through learning. Positive outlook can be imparted through instruction in the event that it is not an inherent trait within an individual. Certain individuals possess an inherent inclination towards embracing the optimistic aspects of existence, while others tend to gravitate towards a more pessimistic orientation. This is additionally shaped by an individual's upbringing and life circumstances.

Positivity, as a cognitive mechanism, involves the deliberate tendency to direct attention towards favorable aspects while selectively disregarding unfavorable ones in certain instances. One can intentionally achieve this by selecting what to concentrate on. Similar to other activities, with continual selection, it will eventually establish a habitual pattern. The brain primarily retrieves information that it frequently engages with. This implies that individuals who habitually fixate on the adverse consequences of situations are more prone to selectively attending to and emphasizing the negative aspects. If such circumstances apply, cultivating optimism will require effort as it entails countering the predominant cognitive processes of the mind. However, it is unquestionably attainable. To achieve this, it will be necessary for you to engage in the deliberate application of the techniques explored in two, which entail the interruption of innate cognitive processes with the objective of governing your cognitive faculties. The process at hand involves actively intervening in situations presenting multiple potential outcomes, wherein one must consciously steer the mind away from fixating on the negative aspects of the choices and instead select to concentrate on the positive facets. Let us revisit the date example presented in two. Suppose you adeptly intervened in your cognitive processes to surmount your apprehension and concluded that you would indeed embark upon the inaugural rendezvous. Prior to your departure, it is possible that you are experiencing apprehension and pondering the potential outcome. Potential outcomes may include a successful date, leading to the expressed interest of the other party in arranging a subsequent encounter. In an alternate scenario, it is possible for the date to be uncomfortable or awkward, leading the other individual to determine that they are not interested in pursuing any further romantic encounters with you. If you do not exhibit tendencies towards optimism, your attention may gravitate towards apprehending the latter consequence. If one possesses an optimistic disposition, it is probable that they will anticipate a favorable outcome prior to the commencement of the event. To acquire an optimistic outlook, it is imperative to cultivate awareness of one's cognitive processes. Please be aware that you are presently fixating on the potential negative consequences. It is advisable to consciously shift your thoughts towards the positive aspects instead. Following repeated practice, this knowledge will gradually permeate your subconscious, fostering an innate anticipation of favorable results. Following a period of time, you will be well on your path towards embracing optimism.

Notwithstanding the potential increase in ease with which you can adopt optimism, it is paramount to bear in mind that there will be occasions when it becomes more challenging, contingent upon the circumstances. Furthermore, it is essential to acknowledge that even those individuals who possess a fundamentally optimistic disposition encounter instances where they struggle to maintain an optimistic outlook. Consequently, they must deliberately engage in cognitive intervention to deliberately choose to direct their thoughts towards the positive aspects.

If one experiences a diminished sense of self-esteem or self-confidence, the practice of optimism may prove to be more challenging. The rationale behind this is that you may hold a strong conviction regarding the high probability and frequency of negative outcomes specifically pertaining to your circumstances, thus facing considerable challenges in persuading yourself otherwise. This is a common characteristic among individuals with diminished self-esteem, and while it may necessitate additional effort on your part, it remains attainable for you to acquire the skill of optimism.

How to Counteract Pessimistic Thoughts" "How to Combat Negative Mindsets" "Strategies for Conquering Negative Thinking" "Techniques for Surmounting Unconstructive Thoughts

Conquering pessimistic thoughts is a significant component in acquiring an optimistic mindset, and presents the utmost challenge within this transformative journey. By opting to direct your attention towards the positive aspects, you are, to some extent, overlooking the negative elements. However, it is undeniable that the negative elements will continue to linger in your subconscious, particularly during the initial stages of acquiring a more optimistic mindset. In the subsequent section, we will explore several strategies for effectively addressing these persistent negative thoughts, particularly those to which one has become habitually inclined to attend. Firstly, we shall commence by examining less efficacious approaches, thereby equipping you with the knowledge of what to avoid.

Ineffective Ways

Suppressing one's thoughts is typically the immediate recourse we opt for when attempting to eliminate negative thoughts, yet it is not the most efficacious approach. When we endeavor to dismiss negative thoughts through resolute efforts, we are still directing our attention towards them. We are directing our efforts towards their elimination, albeit with an unwavering focus on their presence. The human brain is unable to discern between positive and negative thoughts, as they are all perceived as thoughts by the brain. Hence, during our strenuous endeavors to suppress negative thoughts, our minds primarily perceive our intense preoccupation with these thoughts, rendering our attempts to expel them largely futile.

Distraction serves as an alternative approach frequently employed to alleviate our negative thoughts. Engaging in distractions momentarily alleviates our mind from unwanted thoughts; however, once the distraction subsides, these negative thoughts resurface in our consciousness. This can contribute to the reinforcement and exacerbation of thoughts if we persist in our attempts to divert our attention from them.

6) Overcome the sensation of being trapped

Can you envision yourself firmly affixed to your seat? Experience the sensation of being firmly anchored to your chair, with your back secure and your feet firmly planted on the ground. This scenario leaves you with no recourse but to diligently complete your tasks, ensuring their successful and thorough execution. It may be excessive for certain individuals, yet there are those who necessitate additional motivation compared to their counterparts.

7) Let us instill a sense of fear within ourselves for a brief period.

Yes, you comprehend correctly. Experiencing a mild sense of unease does not necessarily entail contemplating a zombie apocalypse scenario beyond our realm of existence, but rather adopting more practical perspectives such as financial concerns. Consider a scenario wherein we find ourselves in a challenging predicament characterized by the accumulation of bills, and our remuneration is not expected until the following fortnight. Occasionally, experiencing a mild scare can serve as a valuable impetus.

Contemplating the repercussions can propel individuals past their thresholds. We have the potential to exploit this sentiment even in the absence of any significant financial considerations. It is akin to constructing a hypothetical scenario that instills a sense of urgency, compelling us to enhance our performance in the actual realm. It is solely psychological in nature, yet the outcomes are exceedingly tangible and highly advantageous.

8) It is imperative that we prioritize self-care and maintain vigilance over our state of well-being.

At times, it can be effortless to disregard our own well-being and the basic factors that can inspire us. The aspect of personal grooming and health can frequently be disregarded, which is consistently deemed as significant. Prior to proceeding with any further actions, it is imperative that we prioritize our personal well-being as our utmost concern.

It is not a matter of greed or anything of that nature, but rather ensuring ourselves that in the event of any adverse circumstances, we possess the ability to proceed at our own discretion. Purchase for ourselves a new suit, a well-presented necktie, and a pair of tasteful footwear or athletic shoes. Engaging in self-investment is always advantageous and sustains personal motivation.

Exercise regimens, along with a nutritious dietary plan, to maintain optimal physical fitness. It is imperative that we do not disregard the importance of our physical well-being. One effective method of enhancing confidence is by maintaining good physical well-being. There is nothing more desirable than possessing a visually appealing and robust physique that both we and others would find captivating. Attaining physical fitness would undoubtedly provide us with an advantageous starting point.

9) Discover the sources of our frequent irritations

Several aspects persistently cause us discomfort. These are the minor aspects that induce an unbearable itch, which truly perturbs us. Determine the nature of the matter and allocate sufficient time for critical analysis, in order to comprehend the circumstances and formulate a strategy to prevent its recurrence.

10) Eliminate Negative Influences

The most perilous phenomenon that we could ever conceive of would be the propagation of negativity. It is excessively detrimental, burdensome, and a complete waste of time. Conversely, it is much simpler to adopt a negative mindset rather than a positive one. Experiencing disillusionment can instigate a multitude of pessimistic ruminations and uncertainties.

It is imperative that we refrain from adopting a negative mindset, as it will invariably divert us from achieving our objectives. In addition, pessimistic thoughts have the potential to deplete our energy and vitality, putting not only our mental well-being but also our physical health in jeopardy.

11) Motivation

Motivation is a crucial component of the formula for achieving success. Our enduring motivation is the impetus that compels us to undertake what is necessary. Discovering the inherent motivation to achieve success holds significant importance, as it is equal in significance to the actual process of taking action. Once we establish our commitment mentally, we can translate it into tangible action in the physical realm.

Motivation serves as an integral element of achieving success, yet it does not stand alone. Motivation in and of itself lacks efficacy without the presence of interconnected elements that constitute the complete framework. Nevertheless, possessing the motivation to undertake tasks is already a considerable accomplishment, yet it still remains incomplete.

12) Dedication and Resolution

Achieving an objective extends beyond mere motivation. While motivation indeed plays a substantial role in the pursuit of a goal, it cannot function in isolation. It must be confronted with equal measures of resolve and dedication.

In order to attain the success we desire, it is imperative that we dedicate ourselves to the achievement of those objectives, displaying unwavering resolve throughout the journey, and possessing the fervor to propel ourselves from initiation to culmination. Whether it pertains to achievement in the workplace, entrepreneurship, or academia, the presence of these three constituents is consistently imperative.

13) Ultimately Attain Contentment with Our Endeavors

Attaining excellence is possible when we discover the pleasure in our work. The optimal approach to accomplishing something is by deriving enjoyment from it. As we strive to attain our objectives, let us derive satisfaction and find delight in the activities we are engaged in. It is solely at that juncture when we can attain excellence and derive satisfaction from our endeavours.

The most exemplary individuals throughout history were never compelled to engage in actions contrary to their volition. They pursued their endeavors out of a deep passion for their craft. They possessed deep ardor, unwavering resilience, extraordinary determination, and unwavering dedication. We could also implement this within our own circumstances.

Every venture commences within our organization, and we initiate our endeavors with a strong drive to attain our objectives. We subsequently achieve our objective with fervor, resolute resolve, and unwavering dedication to excel in life. The paramount aspect is not financial wealth or professional success, but rather the profound sense of joy that permeated our journey from inception to culmination. Enjoy ourselves!

Indications That One Is Evading Accountability For Their Self-Esteem.

Instances of fault, rationalizations, and disavowal (commonly referred to as "BED-time stories") are common indicators that one is failing to assume responsibility for their belief system. These are the narratives in which you divulge to yourself, effectively deterring you from taking action, akin to being in a state of slumber. You can rely on their authenticity, however, they present a distorted representation. Clear manifestations of unwillingness to accept responsibility encompass, yet are not limited to:

Blaming others, your current circumstances, or your personal history

Excessively fixated upon or unwilling to progress further

Exhibiting resistance towards alterations or modifications.

Rationalizing. As an example, phrases such as "exceedingly difficult," "overwhelmingly occupied," or "lacking sufficient funds" may be used.

Possessing a negative victim mentality; harboring thoughts or engaging in discourse indicative of personal injury or disadvantage.

Rejection of matters

Constructing your self-esteem based on external factors, or contingent upon circumstances.

Paralyzing reflections or expressions

Some explicit language or reflections that may serve as cautionary indications include: "

Pretending for the sake of argument

\\\"I can\\\'t\\\"

Life is inherently unpredictable and does not conform to rationality.

If it were within my ability to do so...

\\\"I\\\'m pointless\\\"

I shall do so at the appropriate time.

It is a defect inherent to them.

\\\"Afterward\\\"

These models constitute only a limited selection, and it is probable that you possess your own distinct set of cautionary indicators. It is possible that you are unaware of their existence and subsequently fail to develop an awareness in that regard. Be straightforward with yourself. Initially, you might require assistance from an individual to point out those who stand apart. It is capable of obtaining a genuine and unbiased perspective.

Advice for Embracing Accountability for Your Self-Image

A pivotal development in establishing confidence entails making the decision to assume accountability. Assume ownership and assume accountability for your own life, directing your attention towards it. Revise the bedtime stories to encompass a select few narratives that emphasize ownership, accountability, and duty. That is your decision. Self-assurance originates solely from one's self-perception, and it is within one's own capacity to alter one's thoughts and behaviors. Familiarize yourself with your own indications of notice and observe how you are compromising your own progress. Devote effort towards enhancing your detrimental thoughts and actions. Seek assistance if you require it. Please comprehend that your current capability lies in the present moment and it is incumbent upon you to take action promptly.

Assuming responsibility for your self-assurance is crucial in overcoming low self-esteem. Discover effective strategies for assuming responsibility for your self-worth with the aid of these recommendations.

Certainly, even when setting an attainable objective, it is highly probable that one will end up engaging in repetitive thought patterns or behaviors, while resorting to blame or justifications. You may exhibit resistance to change or encounter challenges in letting go of the past. That is to be expected, as overcoming propensities can be challenging. It is imperative that you make an effort to persevere. Understand that unless you maintain a steadfast commitment to transforming your harmful inclinations, you will remain in your current state indefinitely. In order to make progress, one must acknowledge and let go of the blame and excuses, and instead concentrate on taking action.

It is imperative to exercise self-reflection, particularly if you find it challenging to assume accountability. Mental barriers may impede your progress. Changing deeply ingrained examples can prove to be challenging, as there is a rationale behind the resistance. If you encounter challenges in relinquishing, it is acceptable to seek assistance for your psychological well-being. Requiring adaptation and acknowledging one's potential for substantial impact. Recognize the fact that you are never in solitude.

Just like any comprehensive arrangement, the process of change necessitates a significant investment of time and effort, along with the willingness to explore beyond one's customary boundaries. It is not always easily achievable, but it is somewhat justified irrespective of the level of effort. Assuming responsibility for your belief system is a crucial step in your pursuit of robust self-assurance.

Having a strong sense of self-worth implies that we possess a certain level of influence over the outcomes and events that unfold in our lives. This suggests that we individually take responsibility for our decisions, behavior, and achieving our objectives.

The primary consideration lies in the fact that there is no one who will enhance our lives or protect us. By taking proactive measures and prioritizing self-care, we can elevate our self-esteem. Engaging in self-responsibility represents an active approach to managing both professional obligations and personal life, as opposed to a passive approach. If we fail to engage in practicing self-discipline, we expose ourselves to becoming dependent on other individuals or circumstances.

There are three distinct roles that are commonly fulfilled in a work environment characterized by a lack of personal accountability: the savior, the victim, and the perpetrator. None of these individuals bear any responsibility for their actions. The rescuer is the person who refrains from voicing their true feelings or endeavors to appease everyone, even if it comes at the expense of their own well-being. The rescuer will agree with their superior out of a sense of apprehension about causing any disagreement or fostering animosity. The rescuer assumes responsibility for ensuring the well-being of others and actively endeavors to alleviate their burdens and enhance their overall happiness.

The regrettable consequence befalls the person who perceives themselves as having limited power to alter the situation. This person exhibits unwavering dedication to the role of the saint and thus endeavors to introspectively identify any shortcomings within themselves. The afflicted person will hold the belief that irrespective of their efforts, life invariably fails to yield favorable outcomes. Exploited individuals exhibit signs of self-doubt and remorse.

The individual who alleges against everyone in their vicinity assumes the role of the oppressor. They possess a genuine proficiency in diverting attention away from themselves and are quick to assign blame to others. They will also employ tactics of fear in order to gain compliance. Perpetrators manifest themselves in diverse forms, encompassing those individuals who are distinctively coercive, exerting dominance or subjecting others to humiliation. Furthermore, there exist individuals who employ more nuanced techniques in their endeavors to manipulate or flatter others, with the intent of gaining their support.

Through my interactions with officials and entrepreneurs in counseling sessions, I have observed that seasoned and intellectually adept professionals have acquired valuable insights and knowledge in their respective fields.

They have become aware of the battles that are worth pursuing and those that may tarnish their reputation. They have discovered methods to avoid being led into such circumstances or any of the three careers illustrated. They are steadfast in their approach of either refraining from literal analysis of circumstances or diligently processing their feelings of disappointment or anger. They have successfully learned to moderate their responses.

Younger administrators might still find themselves reacting from an emotional state. One of my clientele consisted of a supervisory executive employed by a divisional manufacturing company that reported to a larger conglomerate. Initially, he demonstrated a high degree of deference in his interactions with his superiors. He consistently advocated for the showcasing of his organization and his behavior.

As we gradually diminished his self-doubt and he grew increasingly self-assured, he began to perceive himself as being on par with his superiors. They soon observed this and commenced advising him on decisions that would impact the broader collective. He transitioned from being a hapless victim to embracing his inherent self-worth and tapping into his inner strength.

All three occupations depicted lack utility both in professional settings and in everyday existence. It is imperative to recognize that each and every one of us bears responsibility for the following:

The fulfillment of our desires or needs

Attaining Cognitive Lucidity: Recommended Actions And Destinations

I remained seated, endeavoring to articulate the reasons behind my desire to solely pursue a career in writing and advance my skills as an author. As I progressed further, my coach posed increasingly thought-provoking inquiries. Subsequently, a flurry of ideas regarding my capabilities flooded my thoughts. Phenomena which escaped my conscious awareness until recently: public speaking and mentoring.

I embarked upon the establishment of a YouTube channel, initiated the creation of a podcast, pursued a coaching academy qualification, became a member of Toastmasters, and experienced a significant amount of delight.

During the process of discussing my actions with my coach, despite encountering difficult inquiries and challenges, I consistently discovered feasible solutions to pursue my passion.

The aforementioned displays the skill of coaching and the adeptness of posing pertinent inquiries. As a result, I have embarked on a path of coaching to facilitate the same sense of fulfillment in others. Upon recognizing the full range of potential available to us, the sensations of enthusiasm and exhilaration may arise. Recognizing our inherent capabilities equates to recognizing our inherent worth. Hence, the utilization of coaching can greatly facilitate personal growth and enhance one's fulfillment as an individual.

What delineates a coach, mentor, and counsellor from one another?

I've summarised below:

A coach is a knowledgeable mentor who can enhance your consciousness, assist you in discerning your authentic desires, and facilitate the exploration of feasible possibilities and strategies to accomplish them.

A mentor can be defined as an individual possessing substantial expertise in the specific field of your interest, who provides direct guidance and recommendations on potential actions.

A counselor is an individual who engages in the examination of your personal history and underlying factors contributing to your emotions, with the objective of enhancing self-awareness. The counsellor or therapist will not proffer solutions, but rather facilitate your process of finding them independently.

Action:

The solution is straightforward in this instance - acquire the assistance of a coach, mentor, or counselor. There are abundant resources available on the internet. It represents a prudent investment without the need for excessive expenditure.

Engaging in discussions regarding various matters is a significant attribute.

I entered my workplace, yet I exhibited a more subdued demeanor than typical. I was not exhibiting my typical demeanor. There was a sense of intrigue surrounding the uncharacteristic behavior displayed by an individual who typically exudes sociability and confidence. I refrained from engaging in any verbal communication.

In the midst of my parents' telephone conversation, I found myself deviating from my customary sociable demeanor and displaying a diminished degree of extroversion. Subsequently, my mother contacted me to inquire about my well-being and overall state, as I had become uncommunicative. Once more, I did not engage in conversation.

During our telephone conversation, my supervisor inquired about my well-being, noting that several individuals had observed me appearing downtrodden and not displaying my typical demeanor. I did not talk.

These and numerous other occurrences in my life resulted in a deep sense of despondency, solitude, and alienation. I found myself surrounded by numerous individuals, yet I was deteriorating internally as a consequence of suppressing my emotions. On certain occasions, I engaged in brief conversations with individuals that momentarily lifted my spirits; however, on subsequent occasions, I reverted to suppressing my feelings of self-doubt.

I came to the realization that it was imperative for me to foster greater self-disclosure and open-mindedness in my interactions with both myself and those around me. I am willing to make any necessary efforts to enhance my self-esteem, and this aspect requires my attention. I am dedicated to significantly boosting my self-esteem, and this entails engaging in more frequent communication.

There have been numerous occurrences in which I have observed individuals undergo a transformation in their demeanor, choosing not to disclose the underlying reasons for their changes. One can only provide limited encouragement for others to engage in conversation, as one ultimately has exclusive control over whether or not they choose to engage in conversation with someone else as well. I have discovered that engaging in discussions regarding personal difficulties has had a profoundly positive impact on my well-being.

I am familiar with this phrase, which I have encountered on multiple occasions, and hold the belief that it holds validity: 'Repression equals depression.'

Indeed, I assert that it is highly self-centered to refrain from engaging in dialogue with an individual when one finds oneself grappling with difficulties. Let me explain...

In instances where individuals choose to withhold and suppress their negative emotions, it is commonly expressed by stating, "I am reluctant to impose my negative thoughts and emotions onto others."

There exist individuals in society who possess a sincere desire to provide assistance, encompassing acquaintances, relatives, and communal networks.

Engaging in the act of suppressing negative thoughts, as I was doing, can be described as:
- Cultivating a pessimistic demeanor that has the potential to adversely affect the morale of those around you (self-centered)
- Instill concern in others about your well-being (self-centered)
- Restricting the manifestation of one's complete state of happiness to the external world (self-centered)
- Failing to divulge one's personal narrative or hardship in order to foster a sense of solidarity among others (self-centered).

This statement does not intend to criticize individuals who consistently suppress their emotions or reflect upon my prior experiences. Rather, it serves as a realization that persistently enduring suffering in solitude causes detriment to both oneself and those in one's vicinity. Furthermore, the advantages of embracing openness extend beyond individual gain.

Thus, may we inquire for assistance?

It could be attributed to the notion of selfishness, whereas in reality, suppressing one's emotions could be perceived as even more self-centered. This reluctance is also influenced by concerns regarding societal judgment and the presence of one's personal ego. The ego constitutes a cognitive component of the human brain responsible for the introspective evaluation of one's personal identity and its perception by external entities.

We are concerned that soliciting assistance may result in the potential impairment of the mentioned item.

May I inquire about the appropriate means of seeking assistance?

Occasionally, I harbored reservations about initiating a request for assistance, as it seemed to entail a substantial leap. Nonetheless, as with most matters, one must indeed undertake concrete measures, lest any substantial alteration remain elusive.

The initial stage was marked by the engagement of a therapist, followed by the subsequent task of outlining the topics for discussion in writing, ultimately culminating in the act of verbal expression during the session.

In our interactions with others, we are leveraging their capabilities as well. The adage "The collective knowledge of multiple individuals surpasses that of a single mind" holds true in all respects. Advancement commences with the recognition of truth and the acceptance of one's need for assistance. It is a universal truth that all individuals require assistance in various forms. Therefore, it is advisable not to dismissively proclaim, "I do not require any help!" Furthermore, it is also strongly recommended to abstain from descending into a state of self-inflicted distress. Seek solace in reaching out and engaging in conversation with others when confronting feelings of confinement or adversity.

Action:

Please make a written record of an issue currently causing significant distress or concern to you.

Next, compile a roster of individuals whom you can repose your trust in to engage in meaningful discussions.

Consequently, make a deliberate effort to engage in a conversation with that individual/those individuals.

There exists no alternative means of enhancing one's conversational skills than actively engaging in conversation with others. It may appear self-evident, yet it serves as a constant reminder.

Implementing Seven Strategies to Eliminate Toxic Elements from Your Lifestyle

1. Analyze Your Situation

Examine your circumstances with scrutiny in order to identify the underlying source of toxicity. As an illustration, endeavor to determine the precise occasion in which you last experienced a sense of tranquility, even if it transpired fleetingly. Did it take place at the residence of your mother? What thoughts were running through your mind during that moment? May I inquire about the location that brings you joy and contentment? How would you describe the sensation of inner harmony? Subsequently, ascertain, within your present circumstances, the elements that are absent in order to attain this state of inner tranquility. If the presence of negativity originates from the individual you cohabit with, it is advisable to thoroughly examine the characteristics and behaviors that contribute to this negativity, and consider strategizing ways in which you can liberate yourself from its influence. If the presence of negativity arises from feelings of tension or stress specifically pertaining to your landlord, it is advisable to explore opportunities to liberate yourself from their influence or to re-evaluate your attachment to them. Immediate action must be taken in response to any form of toxicity. Engaging in procrastination will only serve to amplify the apprehension associated with the detrimental effects.

2. Substitute Negative Elements with Positive Alternatives

After recognizing the detrimental conditions in your life, it is imperative to substitute these adverse circumstances with more favorable ones. As an illustration, in instances where one experiences stress within the confines of their household and struggles to attain a sense of relief, it would prove advantageous to establish a routine of engaging in physical exercise or engaging in fulfilling activities on a daily basis.

3. Discover Your Purpose or a Purpose

Seek out moments of positivity in your life, no matter how insignificant they may seem. If your acquaintances fail to provide the necessary support for your ambitions or if your social circle comprises individuals who exhibit self-centered tendencies that drain your energy, then one potential benefit is that you can take solace in knowing that you do not possess such self-centered qualities. If one perceives oneself as being taken for granted, it is indicative of possessing a heightened capacity for empathy beyond one's self-acknowledgment. This, in turn, allows for the cultivation of self-compassion and the ability to empathize with others in order to discern the favorable aspects.

4. Discover your true calling and cultivate your fervor.

The underlying cause behind the prevalence of negative thoughts and excessive worries, which are often the result of overthinking, is the fact that a significant portion of individuals do not lead lives that align with their deserving or desired circumstances. If one is engaged in a work environment or occupation that is disliked, solely for the purpose of meeting financial obligations, it is indicative of a lack of fulfillment in leading a life driven by passion.

5. Reward yourself often

In times of excessive stress or when a sense of personal equilibrium wanes, it is advisable to allocate a mindful interval to redirect one's focus towards a state of contentment or recollection of pleasant experiences. In doing so, wholeheartedly engage with this moment, relinquishing awareness of external factors and priorities. All other matters can be postponed, for the utmost priority in life is to find personal happiness. When experiencing joy, one's happiness has the potential to evoke a reciprocal response, wherein the world may also manifest a smile. Frequently engage in nature walks, as this enables your mind to absorb the sights and scents of the natural environment, which possess remedial effects.

6. Embrace and accept errors.

Take into account that there will be no prompt alteration. Transformation occurs in the lives of numerous individuals, and with increased dedication and diligence, one's mastery will inevitably progress. Occasionally, the extent of change might not be as readily discernible as we desire. Every individual experiences challenging days, therefore, during these periods, it is imperative to display self-compassion and acknowledge that it is acceptable to encounter consecutive instances of such days. Acknowledge that errors are an inevitable part of the process and that experiencing setbacks is the sole means to progress. We do not derive our knowledge from our healthy habits; rather, our mistakes serve as valuable lessons that impart new insights and reinforce the importance of cultivating positive habits.

7. Seek Professional Help

In moments when circumstances appear unfavorable, errors persistently arise, and one's sense of regression surpasses their initial standing, seeking the aid of a professional often proves most fruitful. Professionals such as therapists, medical practitioners, naturopaths, and clinical counselors possess the expertise to guide you effectively while equipping you with valuable coping strategies to initiate a journey towards cultivating positivity. Frequently, the predominance of anxiety or mood disorders impairs cognitive functioning, making it increasingly arduous to muster the motivation to rise and embrace each day. Perhaps it is worth considering that the underlying issue lies not solely within your thoughts, but rather stems from a more profound source. Exclusively a skilled expert possesses the competency to guide you out of your predicament and set you back on the trajectory towards attaining your desired objectives.

Eliminating toxicity from our lives is of utmost importance as it can bear us down and serve as a catalyst for further pessimistic thoughts. Failing to address or proactively eliminate toxicity deprives us of a justifiable opportunity to thrive.

Step 4: Prepare to Embrace Transformation

Have you ever experienced a tendency to excessively fixate on either future prospects or past events? This is a practice in which many individuals frequently engage. Nevertheless, it is important to acknowledge that the individual you were five years ago or will become five years henceforth exhibits a significant dissimilarity to the person you presently are.

It can be observed that half a decade ago, your preferences, inclinations, and social circle differed from what they presently are, and it is likely that they will undergo further transformations in the forthcoming five years. The crucial aspect is to acknowledge and embrace one's current self, while recognizing that one continues to actively evolve.

Based on the findings derived from Carol Dweck's research, it becomes evident that academic achievement amongst children significantly improves when they embrace a growth-oriented perspective. Indeed, individuals with a growth mindset hold the belief that they are capable of performing admirably in a specific academic discipline. This starkly contrasts with the experience of children with a fixed mindset, as they firmly hold the belief that their inherent qualities and possessions are unchangeable. Consequently, embracing the belief that one is incapable of personal growth significantly undermines their self-assurance.

To fully embrace your true self, it is imperative to cease engaging in self-criticism. Often, our tendency is to assess individuals based on their language, manner of expression, attire, and behavior. Likewise, we assess ourselves mentally by drawing comparisons between our former and current selves.

In order to cultivate a robust sense of confidence, it is imperative that you commence by overcoming the tendency to engage in self-evaluation and indulge in unfavorable critique. Indeed, this can pose as a formidable challenge initially, yet as one engages in diligent application, it becomes evident how regressive such a course of action was.

You may initiate this process by electing to refrain from passing any judgments for a minimum of one or two days per week. If you are unable to provide constructive or positive input, it is advisable to refrain from making any remarks. In the event that a pessimistic thought enters your mind, seek to substitute it with a constructive one.

Over time, your mind will progressively acclimate to a state devoid of judgment, eventually transforming into your innate state of mind. This will not only facilitate the acceptance of others, but also foster self-acceptance in alignment with one's authentic self.

Step 5: Cultivate Mindfulness
Sounds simple, right? It is imperative and indispensable that you cultivate your confidence. By maintaining your presence, you are effectively enabling your mind, body, and soul to be fully active and occupied with the task at hand.

Let us consider the scenario of conversing with an individual who displays a lack of receptiveness towards our discourse. This is an occurrence that has likely transpired for a substantial portion of individuals. How did you feel? Alternatively, consider a scenario where you engage in a conversation with an individual and experience an overwhelming sense of being the sole focus of their attention, completely disregarding the presence of others in the vicinity. Feels pretty special, huh?

The rationale behind your sense of being extraordinary resides in their presence during that particular instance. They diligently attended to your words, profoundly empathizing with every sentiment expressed. They were actively involved in the discussion on a more profound level. By adopting this approach, you can effectively retain information without compromising your ability to empathize.

In order to guarantee one's presence, it is crucial to cultivate a cognitive method of verification. This implies that one should consistently engage in self-reflection and self-evaluation. In order to accomplish this, it is imperative to cultivate a cognitive prompt or schedule by which you inquire into the state of your mind. This is the juncture at which you assume the role of a dispassionate observer of your own psyche.

Are you contemplating making dinner reservations during the course of our meeting? Do you believe that your abilities are insufficient? To disengage from these negative thoughts implies periodically engaging in introspection to assess one's mental state. Upon obtaining the solution to your inquiry, inhale deeply and refocus your attention on the utmost priorities in your life.

The Profound Influence Of Self-Assurance

Allow me to disclose a confidential piece of information to you. This information remains confidential as it is often met with reluctance by many individuals to acknowledge. The truth of the matter is that a significant number of individuals are uncertain and lacking in self-assurance. Now, please endeavor to maintain a composed state of mind. The absence of firm conviction does not necessarily imply a complete absence of self-assurance. They lack enough confidence. Stated differently, it falls beneath the threshold necessary for them to thrive and achieve optimal levels of performance in their everyday lives.

Now, this disclosure is evidently clear. By thoroughly analyzing the lives of individuals within your acquaintance, it can be affirmed with a high degree of certainty that, in approximately 80% of instances, they are failing to actualize their utmost capabilities. To put it differently, they possess immense potential but opt to lead a life that falls significantly short of realizing that potential. They are being compensated; they are being relegated to second position. They are not fully embracing the opportunities available to them in order to maximize their potential in life.

Once more, the underlying cause can be attributed to their deficiency in self-assurance. They lack the necessary level of confidence. This is the reason why individuals who exhibit substantial levels of self-assurance are highly captivating. Individuals who are deficient in self-assurance tend to gravitate towards individuals who exude certainty. Now, try to contain your enthusiasm. The positive aspect of this is readily apparent; it is effortless to perceive individuals who are attracted to you, and they offer you encouragement. The underlying premise, regardless of their verbal expression, is that I am drawn to you due to a particular quality you possess, which I lack to a significant degree.

Nevertheless, it is also possible to elicit negative attention from individuals. Certain individuals may possess a deficit in self-assurance and possess an awareness of this shortcoming. Consequently, they may endeavor to engage in acts of criticism, revelation, or confrontation aimed at individuals who naturally exude higher levels of confidence. There consistently exists a degree of variation.

Ultimately, it can be concluded that regardless of the manifestation, individuals who possess self-assurance are highly captivating due to their ability to instill a sense of ease in those around them. Additionally, an adverse magnetic effect can occur as individuals may experience feelings of envy towards one's possessions. Their desire for personal comfort notwithstanding, they perceive that their sole recourse to compensate for their own insecurity is by adopting an offensive stance towards others.

However, one will exude an irresistible charm once imbued with self-assurance. It is true that individuals frequently meet the expectations or desires of others in order to provide solace and assistance. Put differently, those in your vicinity are seeking guidance and authoritative direction. They exhibit the behavior of disoriented sheep in search of a guiding shepherd. I understand that this statement may appear offensive because if one were to directly tell someone that they are behaving like a sheep, it would not be unexpected to receive a physical response in return.

Nevertheless, it is an undeniable reality that individuals, to varying degrees, experience a dearth of self-assurance and possess an awareness of this fact. This is the reason why they instinctively are attracted to individuals who possess a robust level of conspicuously evident and easily discernible self-assurance. Why does this happen? What is the underlying reason behind the pursuit of effective leadership? Indeed, individuals who exude confidence have the remarkable ability to instill a sense of possibility in those around them. This embodies the essence of effective leadership. When you cultivate an environment in which others perceive the feasibility of certain endeavors, you become an irresistible figure in their midst. Why? When granted autonomy or in the absence of external intervention, they tend to perceive tasks as being more challenging than they truly are. They hold the belief that circumstances are challenging and that numerous hindrances present themselves throughout the journey.

When you make your presence felt and ignite their inspiration, and they perceive the potential for success, they naturally cannot resist but to be alert and attentive. You stimulate their intellectual faculties to contemplate matters beyond their usual cognition. When one spends a considerable amount of time amidst individuals who possess self-assurance, they have the tendency to influence others into perceiving not just the feasibility, but rather the likelihood of various outcomes. This embodies the qualities and traits that individuals seek in effective leadership. This is the desired attribute that individuals are seeking within their social networks.

Have you ever observed collectives of adolescents wherein certain individuals exhibit a higher propensity towards aggression compared to their peers? When one assembles a cohort of adolescent males, typically characterized by timidity, and introduces an equally youthful leader who incites and inspires them toward prescribed objectives, the ensuing outcomes can be remarkably astonishing. Indeed, this situation can yield either favorable or unfavorable outcomes.

Many instances of hooligan violence and gang violence, frequently reported in the media, often revolve around groups of adolescents who are influenced by one or a couple of leaders, instilling in them a belief that certain actions are not only feasible but highly likely to occur. Engage in theft from an establishment specializing in the sale of alcoholic beverages? Indeed, if the leader is not involved, then that notion becomes mere wishful thinking. Once an individual of suitable caliber is introduced into their midst, it is merely a question of time until the collective endeavors of the group lead to the successful execution of a robbery at a liquor store.

Are you able to perceive the mechanics of this process? This can result in either positive or negative outcomes. However, it is an undeniable fact that individuals who possess confidence have the ability to instill in those around them a sense that not only are things achievable, but that success is highly likely. I cannot speak for you, but in my view, that epitomizes the concept of power.

What strategies can be implemented to mitigate social anxieties?

Breathing exercises

Respiration is among the limited number of bodily functions that the human body executes utilizing both the conscious and subconscious faculties. The conscious regulation of subconscious breathing is an immensely potent technique. An initial indication of anxiety is a heightened rate of superficial respiration. This may occur when you are on the verge of attending the event. It may also occur when contemplating the occurrence. When you perceive this phenomenon occurring, it is advisable to endeavor to regain authority over your respiration. For instance, In the event that you sense an inclination of nervousness or apprehension emerging in relation to a particular social circumstance, it would be advisable to locate a seat and engage in the subsequent breathing technique: "

1. Please assume a comfortable seated position, ensuring that your back is upright and your gaze is directed forward. Please place your right hand upon your right thigh and position your left hand upon the upper region of your abdomen.

2. Inhale gradually through your nasal passages, allowing your abdomen to expand as the air enters your lungs. Ensure that you dedicate a minimum of 4 seconds to draw in a breath. Retain the breath for a duration of 2 seconds prior to gradually releasing it. Exhale through your mouth. It is expected that the exhalation of all the air from your lungs would require more than 4 seconds.

3. It is recommended that you engage in this activity for a duration of 2 minutes, or until a sense of relaxation is achieved. After completion of the task, all instances of rapid and superficial breathing should have ceased.

Mitigate anxiety-induced behavior through the implementation of strategies aimed at subduing fear.

After the trigger, the flight response tends to become entrenched as a habitual pattern for the majority of individuals. Initially, a socially anxious introvert may endeavor to persuade oneself to attend the gathering. With the passage of time, the individual ceases to contemplate attending. Whenever the prospect of attending an event evokes discomfort within him, he invariably opts against going.

It is possible to modify this habit, despite years of its consistent practice. Your task simply involves discerning the catalyst for your fear and subsequently providing a comprehensive account of the ensuing actions. Subsequently, it is crucial to discern the gratifying sensation that ensues when one chooses to abstain from attending an occasion due to apprehension.

Having recognized the recurring pattern of your habit, it is imperative for you to establish a negative association with this behavior. Consider the detrimental consequences associated with the particular habit. Create a comprehensive inventory to serve as a reminder of the adverse consequences that your habit has inflicted upon you. This will effectively persuade your subconscious that the habit is not yielding any favorable outcomes for you.

Subsequently, it is imperative to consider implementing a modification in behavior as a result of the identified trigger. As previously indicated, the initial stage involves the trigger. It is subsequently accompanied by the regularity of the practice. The sensation of being triggered and the accompanying fear will consistently endure. You cannot change that. It is possible to modify the ensuing behavior resulting from the feeling of fear. Suppose you consistently refrain from attending familial holiday dinners due to a certain unpleasant incident. Each instance in which you ponder the occurrence, you experience an internal sensation of embarrassment. Over the course of time, this sentiment has evolved into apprehension regarding the potential recurrence of a similar encounter in subsequent instances.

You are required to make a decision to proceed. It is imperative that you refrain from engaging in self-debate or vacillating over the decision of whether to proceed or abstain. Once you have made the determination to attend the subsequent event, your ensuing obstacle will entail contending with the ruminations that will evoke recollections of your distressing and mortifying encounter. In order to mitigate its influence on your decision-making process, it is advisable to seek alternative strategies to modify your behavior whenever recollections of the aforementioned experiences emerge in your consciousness.

Rather than excessively pondering the matter, one could articulate the phrase "I am departing" and redirect their thoughts towards an alternative idea.

Whenever your apprehension towards social gatherings arises, it is advisable to recite this particular utterance. Expressing it in words instills a perception of resilience in the majority of individuals. It signifies the modification in behavior that will permanently restore their participation in social gatherings.

Finally, it is imperative to promptly identify the trigger when it materializes. Each instance you experience fear, commence the process of foreseeing the subsequent conduct. It is advisable to employ the aforementioned phrase or any suitable alternative in order to avoid your mind developing the aforementioned pattern.

Engage in the exploration of apprehensive thoughts.

Confronting fear is regarded as one of the most effective methods to address it. One might experience a sense of being overwhelmed if they were to confront all of their fears simultaneously. It would be more prudent to confront them individually. Rather than attending every social engagement to which you are invited, it would be more prudent to direct your attention towards a singular event. After having participated in the aforementioned event, it is advisable to contemplate your future attendance at the subsequent gathering. It is imperative to ensure oneself that the worst-case scenario conjured in the mind is invariably a manifestation of irrational fear and is highly unlikely to materialize.

After participating in numerous social gatherings, you will gradually develop an appreciation for the experience. The cultivation of courage will initiate as apprehensions surrounding an event arise. As one attends a greater number of events, the propensity to attend them gradually takes shape. When the aforementioned habit becomes ingrained, a transformative effect occurs, as one's confidence undergoes a discernible positive evolution. The crucial factor lies in altering one's habits.

2.4 Relationships

Having a strong sense of self-assurance is integral to fostering and maintaining healthy relationships. Whether you are referring to a romantic liaison, familial ties, or friendships, it necessitates self-assurance to embody one's true self within the context of any relationship. Having the self-assurance to fully embrace your identity and genuinely acknowledge the complexities of the circumstances is essential in fostering a more profound interpersonal bond.

The cultivation of positive thinking will significantly enhance one's level of confidence. Confidence is an intangible quality that presents challenges when attempting to quantify or cultivate. It originates from the depths of the soul, with the innate understanding that individuals hold the power to ensure their own personal safety and well-being. Confidence comes from self-security. If one has a multitude of elements that they carry as objects of shame, such as previous encounters or other causes of humiliation, it becomes challenging for them to cultivate a sense of self-assurance. In order to possess confidence, it is imperative to release all extraneous concerns and acknowledge internally that you possess inherent worth as an individual who deserves attention, appreciation, and comprehension, and subsequently convey your thoughts and feelings with such self-assurance.

The optimal and exemplary approach to exude self-assurance is to embrace your authentic self and assertively embrace it. Embrace your height with pride and confidently showcase it to the world, should you possess the gift of being tall. If one happens to possess a diminutive stature, it is imperative to embrace and wholeheartedly appreciate this quality. There exists a vast array of bodily characteristics, and there exists a diverse range of individuals who hold an affinity for individuals possessing traits similar to yours. Regardless of the personal qualities or attributes that you may feel insecure about, it is essential to abandon these anxieties and release them. It will prove advantageous for your future endeavors.

2.5 Intuition

Intuition can be considered an abstract notion. There is no alternative methodology for examining it, save for soliciting individuals to elucidate their encounters with intuition. Intuition can be regarded as the fusion of one's spiritual, physical, and cognitive aspects, harmoniously converging into a unified whole. It considers the emotions, cognitive processes, and somatic responses that you undergo, subsequently guiding you towards the most appropriate course of action.

Intuition is an inherently human phenomenon that defies simple explanation. It does not constitute anxiety, fear, or any particular emotional state. Instead, it is the amalgamation of sentiment, cognition, and perception that enables individuals to arrive at reasoned judgments. When you experience a sense of intuition, endeavor to heed its guidance. Certain individuals may lack an understanding of the sensation associated with being able to heed one's intuition. They may even be oblivious to the subtle indications or cues pertaining to a particular situation or individual.

Intuition can be described as that instinctive sensation that someone is being untruthful, or that subtle pang in the abdomen when one becomes aware of achieving a prize. The physiological response precedes cognitive recognition. The human body is a remarkably intelligent entity; while it is commonly believed in Western societies that the mind is solely responsible for intelligence, this notion only holds partially true. The physical embodiment contributes significantly to our innate sensations and intuitive cognitive processes, acting as a reliable indicator of both potential harm and deceit. It serves as an indicator when an individual requires sincere assistance or when we experience the emotion of love. The mind is a realm inhabited by thoughts and ideas, whereas the body houses concrete sensory data that holds greater reliability compared to thoughts.

Contemplate the most recent occurrence of your dream state. Did you have knowledge that it was a dream? Probably not. There have been accounts of individuals who claim to possess the ability to exert control over their dreams through a phenomenon commonly referred to as lucid dreaming. In this procedure, an individual can bring to their awareness during sleep that they are actively participating in a dream state, thereby recognizing that the contents of their imagination are purely illusory. Once individuals acquire this ability, they will be able to subsequently guide their actions within the realm of the dream. They can gradually assert greater control over their emotions and thoughts, thereby acquiring the ability to consciously vocalize during their dream states.

A significant majority of individuals, however, lack proficiency in this particular skill, which is entirely customary. They perceive their dreams as entirely tangible to their reality. During instances of dreaming, individuals encounter difficulty in discerning reality, resulting in a tendency to wholeheartedly accept the veracity of dream content, regardless of its fantastical or implausible nature. In this state, they genuinely perceive and ascribe truth to the events unfolding within the dream, firmly believing in their occurrence.

This illustration exhibits the inherent unreliability of our cognitive faculties. If one possesses the capacity to create an alternate realm wherein concepts like flight or other utterly implausible phenomena are possible, it is intriguing to contemplate the boundless extents to which one's cognitive faculties can diverge in the realm of daily contemplation. The body exhibits a relatively low degree of fallibility. The human body does not engage in cognitive thought processes; rather, it simply responds instinctively. The human body serves as a domain where one lacks control over its occurrences, and it is within these parameters that the essence of truth manifests. The veracity lies within the realm of nonverbal communication, as the body instinctively responds. There exists an absence of a cognitive filtration mechanism.

When you experience a particular sentiment towards someone through your intuition, endeavor to acknowledge the validity of that perception. It may not align with your immediate inclination, but it is worth acknowledging the legitimacy of your somatic intuition; subsequently, you can begin to effectively harness these insights. A great number of individuals develop the habit of disregarding their intuition as they mature, influenced by a multitude of factors. One compelling rationale for this is that they were instilled with the notion of suppressing their emotions during their formative years. Numerous individuals belonging to the younger generation, who have been raised by parents with stringent tendencies, exhibit such behavior. As children, they were instilled with the belief that showing or verbalizing emotions renders them feeble, and hence, they are discouraged from expressing their feelings due to the apprehension of being deserted or subjected to criticism. This formative experience is highly detrimental and significantly impacts an individual's capacity to place confidence in their instincts. In order for an individual of this nature to cultivate the capacity for relying on their intuition, possessing a sense of confidence will prove to be instrumental.

This is an individual displaying a diminished sense of self-worth. An individual who possesses diminished self-esteem may encounter difficulties in placing confidence in their intuition, as they have acquired or convinced themselves that their instincts are unreliable. This notion does not hold true, as the validity of one's inner feelings applies universally. Consequently, it is imperative for this individual to acquire self-assurance. Exposure therapy proves to be advantageous in this regard. According to the tenets of exposure therapy, prolonged exposure to stimuli that elicit discomfort enables individuals to acquire effective coping mechanisms. Furthermore, you will gradually develop a greater capacity to endure prolonged periods of stimulation, as you become more adept at handling intense situations, metaphorically speaking.

Consequently, individuals grappling with self-assurance concerns ought to seek opportunities that lie beyond their usual sphere of familiarity. First and foremost, you may consider positioning yourself in a manner that enables you to undertake calculated ventures. If an individual experiences social anxiety, they may consider seeking employment at a coffee shop or a similar venue that entails moderate interaction with a considerable number of individuals. This will prompt you to consider ways to engage with individuals, fostering a gradual sense of ease and familiarity with daily social interactions. The greater the number of individuals with whom you engage, the more apparent it becomes that you possess qualities which are unique and intriguing when you approach such interactions with sincerity. Subsequently, a sense of assurance will develop and flourish.

Strategies for Conquering Fear

This poses a significant inquiry, given the multitude of fear variations that individuals may encounter, each person exhibiting unique manifestations of such fears. In the following segment, our attention will be directed towards apprehensions pertaining to self-assurance and one's sense of value, such as anxiety over public performance, trepidation in novel circumstances, the dread of social ostracism, and similar concerns.

The initial strategy we shall explore for individuals with diminished self-assurance or self-regard when endeavoring to conquer fear involves directing conscious attention to one's mental state and its focal point. This implies that at any given instance, our cognitive processes are directed towards specific thoughts or topics, and we frequently fail to discern them due to their rapid and ever-changing nature. The crucial aspect lies in being mindful of our thoughts and being observant of their target of focus. Our current objective is to foster awareness by emphasizing the need to observe and acknowledge existing circumstances, as this is pivotal in bringing about any form of alteration. By attentively observing one's thoughts and directing one's focus, it becomes possible to intervene in the subconscious processing of thoughts. Consequently, individuals can implement modifications prior to fear gaining control. You shall commence by directing your focus towards your thoughts at sporadic intervals throughout the day, in order to acclimate yourself to discerning your involuntary cognitions and alterations in awareness. Once you acquire proficiency in this task, you will enhance your ability to perform it during moments of heightened agitation, such as instances characterized by fear. When experiencing fear, one is capable of directing attention towards introspection, enabling the identification of the underlying causes inducing such fear. Subsequently, you may allocate sufficient time to contemplate your thoughts, thereby enabling yourself to arrive at a more informed and judicious resolution pertaining to a given circumstance, as opposed to hastily determining one's course of action solely driven by fear-induced anxieties. As previously mentioned, when one succumbs to fear, they experience the instinctive fight or flight response, which obliterates the capacity for rational thought, cognitive analysis, and deliberation of advantages and disadvantages, as it is centered solely on ensuring survival. Below, I will provide you with an illustration of what this entails.

Upon encountering your former romantic partner at the subway station, your physiological and psychological faculties are swiftly consumed by a formidable surge of apprehension, prompting an instinctual response of either seeking flight or engaging in a confrontational exchange.

Typically, one would instinctively react without contemplating the situation, leading to an immediate choice between approaching the individual to engage in conflict or hastily retreating up the stairs to withdraw from the scene. Nevertheless, a more appropriate course of action would entail acknowledging and addressing the sensation of apprehension when it arises. Instead of succumbing to it, it is advised to take a moment to inhale deeply, and consciously observe that your mind is compelling you to either engage in conflict or evade the situation. Observing this phenomenon constitutes the initial stage. Through the deliberate engagement of this automated procedure within your conscious awareness, you can enhance your ability to regulate it effectively.

Subsequently, you shall allocate a few moments in order to deliberate upon the circumstances and establish a well-reasoned judgement, as opposed to succumbing to fear and allowing your instinctual mind and physical responses to guide your choices.

In order to systematically analyze the situation, it is necessary to reflect upon the most recent encounter with the involved individuals, evaluate the nature of that interaction, consider one's current sentiments towards them, and ascertain the objectives desired from this particular encounter. Subsequently, after undertaking this action and attaining tranquility by taking a few measured breaths, you can deliberate on whether to approach her and offer greetings or to proceed along the platform to board a separate subway car, thereby circumventing any interaction with her.

Observe the transition from the options of engaging in a conflict or fleeing, to the options of initiating a polite interaction or boarding the subway at the opposite terminal. Gone are the primal instincts of fight or flight; instead, a new paradigm presents itself, offering two deliberate and reasoned courses of action. After careful consideration, it is possible that there exist additional alternatives beyond a mere two. In the event of a distressing separation, it may be advisable to temporarily vacate the subway station until the departure of the train, returning subsequently. It is advisable to greet from a distance and refrain from further interaction. By engaging in careful deliberation for a few moments, one can generate alternatives and deliberately select the most suitable option according to individual requirements and personal level of ease, rather than being driven by a reactive fear.

Through diligently cultivating an observant mindset towards one's thoughts and internal cognitive processes during automatic behaviors, one can subsequently attain heightened awareness in fear-inducing situations, thereby effectively intervening in the instinctual fight or flight response. In order to enhance your proficiency in this matter, endeavor to observe your thoughts on multiple occasions throughout the day for a duration of time, thus familiarizing yourself with the sensation of bringing your subconscious thoughts into your conscious awareness.

Suggestions To Enhance Motivation

All ofushavesome form of motivationFurthermore, it varies individually for each of us. There are certain factors that have the potential to inspire us, such as the acquisition of a high-quality pair of shoes, engaging in recreational shopping, or simply having some leisure time at our disposal. Regardless of the cause of our motivation, there exist certain factors that help sustain our sense of motivation.

In spite of your diligent endeavors towards achieving success in life, there are occasions when our motivation appears to plummet abruptly. These circumstances are quite typical, and fortunately, there exist uncomplicated methods to circumvent them.

1) Imagination

If an idea can be conceived, it can be accomplished. It has been asserted that whether one believes one is capable or incapable, one's belief is correct.

Imagination serves as an inexhaustible wellspring of knowledge. It is the prime motivator behind individuals' inclination to innovate and devise novel solutions to enhance the quality of life. It also serves as the inception point for motivation. Envisioning the commencement of events, the orchestrated sequence, and the desired outcomes are likely to serve as the driving force behind individuals' intentions.

However, there is one caveat to this nonetheless. We must refrain from indulging in pessimistic thoughts or counterproductive imaginations that could have a detrimental impact. The capacity of a pessimistic imagination is limited in its ability to foster uncertainty. It would yield no benefits and offer no motivation whatsoever.

Conversely, embracing an awareness of repercussions can be beneficial. Please refrain from pursuing a course of action that would jeopardize the integrity of our entire motivational scheme. Maintain a positive mindset and envision grander possibilities that will ignite our spirits and inspire ourselves.

2) Cultivating Consistent Motivation

As long as there is breath within us, there remains promise of attaining remarkable accomplishments. While we may have achieved certain objectives, it should not be mistaken as the culmination of our existence wherein no further stimulation or drive is required.

We must bear in mind that in the absence of motivation, forward progress would be unattainable. Inculcate motivation as a daily practice. Envision, reenvision, and experience our thoughts. By consistently incorporating this practice into our daily routine, we will effortlessly attain an improved existence, reach unprecedented accomplishments, and evolve into a superior individual.

3) Commence each morning with a positive mindset

Have you ever awakened on the incorrect side of the bed? The majority of individuals have experienced this phenomenon at some point, and its duration persisted for the entirety of the day. Just as negativity has the potential to persist from the instant we arise until we retire for the evening, so too can maintaining a positive outlook. Begin the day positively by greeting it with a warm smile and adopting a positive demeanor. Having the appropriate mindset at the opportune moment can significantly alter the outcome.

Finally, there are no justifiable grounds that hinder us from promptly electing to alter the fundamental sentiment pertaining to our sense of self. Additionally, it is imperative to acknowledge that our individual flaws contribute to our humanity. In the event that all of our imperfections and shortcomings were to abruptly dissipate, it is my conjecture that we would instantaneously metamorphose into pure luminosity, ultimately ceasing to exist within the realm of this planet. By adopting this perspective, as we strive for true self-acceptance, it may be crucial for us to embrace our imperfections with a sense of particular satisfaction. Given all factors taken into account, if we were completely exempt from criticism, we would never have the opportunity to rise to this exceptionally challenging ordeal.

Continuing to Live Mindfully

When one continues with an intentional existence, they are inevitably destined to lead a fulfilled and contented real-life experience, brimming with joy and happiness. Continuing with a mindful existence entails carefully evaluating one's actions, decisions, and choices. You are making deliberate choices based on your values and personal integrity.

What is conscious life?

Living consciously entails purposeful and meticulously deliberated existence. It involves introspection followed by making informed choices.

It is intriguing to ponder the reasoning behind your actions, by carefully considering the intentions driving each decision you make. It is not aimlessly drifting within the current of existence, but rather executing a conscious and determined maneuver.

Imagine entering a shop without prior knowledge of your intended purchase. Living intentionally involves deliberating over a fundamental inventory of food items and determining the course of action for dinner preparations this week. Living consciously is akin to making the necessary arrangements and preparations, such as securing a flight ticket well in advance, determining the specific airline of choice, and identifying the intended destination, prior to arriving at the airport terminal.

Unexpectedly, the overwhelming majority do not adhere to this lifestyle. They adhere to established norms, familial expectations, or conform to societal directives.

What are the benefits of living with intention?

Typically, we do not often have the chance to lead a mindful existence. Throughout the entirety of our existence, from the moment of conception until our final breath, our actions are predetermined. Our parents foster in us a particular identity, influencing our preferences for certain food and guiding our career choices. Society reveals to us that success stems from residing in a specific locality, attaining a professional degree, procuring a certain type of abode, or driving a particular automobile.

In addition to familial and societal spheres, global organizations are actively pursuing our financial resources in order to market their products and fulfill the expectations of stakeholders. By purposefully leading your life, you are able to confront and question all aspects. One can exercise prudent judgement by declining things that do not align with one's values or beliefs.

Comparisons

I started university. I had highly anticipated it with great enthusiasm. So many possibilities. Engaging in social interactions, participating in football activities, and experiencing the nuances of daily life within a unfamiliar urban setting, namely Sheffield.

I participated in freshers' week in 2009 and thoroughly enjoyed the experience.

Engaging in social gatherings and recreational activities with acquaintances within the confines of my residence has afforded me with a degree of experience. Furthermore, I would like to add that if you intend to invest time in developing your abilities, it would be more beneficial to focus on enhancing your interpersonal aptitude rather than honing your capacity for consuming alcoholic beverages.

However, I soon discovered that during the initial few weeks of my experience, the gentlemen in my vicinity were engaging in the pursuit of engaging with young ladies and subsequently accompanying them back to their accommodations. These individuals appeared to be highly esteemed among their peers. I was insufficiently self-assured to engage in conversations with the girls, however. Thus, what was the method I employed to tackle this issue?

Rather than devoting more time to improving myself, I began attempting to emulate the appearance of these gentlemen. Although my appearance was not unattractive, I was completely unfamiliar with the art of imitating their fashion.

I gradually grew disillusioned with myself.

I underwent a transformation in which I distanced myself from my former identity due to a lack of self-esteem.

Additionally, there existed an individual named Adam who excelled in athletics.

Adam was a proficient athlete who maintained a continuous momentum in his running endeavors, and his coach consistently provided positive reinforcement regarding his commendable performance. He would derive a sense of gratification from it, yet upon witnessing individuals of his age accomplishing significantly superior times, he commenced harboring skepticism regarding his own capabilities.

He consistently attended the running sessions, however, he gradually started to experience a declining sense of pleasure.

When engaging in comparisons with others, our locus of control is restricted to matters within our own sphere of influence.

By diverting our attention away from ourselves, we consequently divert our attention away from the essence of our identity.

As a result, it is imperative that we shift our focus towards ourselves.

Enjoy improving yourself. Enjoy trying your best.

Take pleasure in engaging in activities that align with your personal preferences and contribute to a sense of self-fulfillment. All of these factors are within your jurisdiction.

In subsequent chapters, I delve into the utilization of a role model as a means of fostering confidence. It can prove beneficial to assimilate certain positive qualities, yet one should refrain from attempting to emulate another individual. Embrace your individuality, for there is no need to conform when others have already done so.

The preeminent statement I must convey regarding comparisons, as well as various other facets explored in the book, pertains to the notion of self-acceptance. In order to initiate progress, it is necessary for you to acknowledge and accept your current circumstances. It pertains to acknowledging your current circumstances and actively investing in self-improvement. When we evade our own actuality, we are conveying to ourselves a message that we harbor a profound dissatisfaction towards our own being. We aspire to emulate another individual. How do you believe this contributes to the development of our self-esteem?

Action:

Record your daily accomplishments in a journal. By making a conscious record of 3-5 accomplishments I attain on a daily basis, it significantly aids in uplifting my mood and instills within me a sense of pride for my accomplishments. There is no obligation for you to undertake significant actions. Examples could include engaging in physical exercise, taking a leisurely stroll, delivering a comprehensive status report during a meeting, or engaging in a myriad of other activities.

Instances of noteworthy accomplishments to document in a personal journal at the end of each day:

A pleasant stroll

● Offering praise to someone else ● Extending a compliment to another individual ● Expressing admiration for someone else ● Offering words of approval or admiration to another person ● Recognizing and commending someone else

● Engaging in a meaningful dialogue with someone

● Participating in fitness activities at the gym

- Participating in a training session for a sports team
- Engaging in a challenging task in the professional setting
- Contemplative practice
- Engaging in the rehearsal of a public presentation
- Engaging in the practice of keeping a journal
- Successfully completing a household responsibility that has been delayed.

An alternative phrase for expressing the same idea in a formal tone could be: "An supplementary practice entails integrating fresh convictions into your mindset." This behavior can be observed when individuals perceive themselves as inadequate, prompting them to engage in comparisons with others. The utilization of the affirmation "I possess sufficient worthiness and incredible qualities" has greatly facilitated my journey towards embracing and appreciating my true self.

I utter it at minimum thrice daily, allotting a few minutes per occasion.

It entails the incorporation of a message within the depths of my subconscious. Therefore, uttering these words to oneself can yield significant advantages. It may not yield immediate outcomes, however, over time, you will begin to adopt a sincere belief and emotional experience of it. What have you got to lose? Modifying one's mindset requires a minimal exertion of energy.

Seek Changes

This is the stage where diligent efforts culminate in tangible outcomes. This is the pivotal moment when you must proactively initiate these modifications, thereby facilitating progress towards your aspirations or the desired trajectory of your life. There are numerous possibilities for occurrence, yet there are a handful of prevailing patterns. Several frequently utilized approaches for overcoming negative thoughts include:

Therapy

Various modalities of therapy offer the opportunity to rectify cognitive processes, thereby enabling individuals to enhance their psychological well-being. Occasionally, one may find great value in having a reliable guiding presence that can assist in unraveling the complexities of one's tasks and emotions. With the aid of such assistance, individuals may gradually uncover improved methods for addressing various circumstances. This can also prove advantageous if you discover that you are encountering difficulties in advancing independently or if you ascertain the necessity of devising a more effective approach to address the challenges in your immediate environment. With the assistance of a therapist, you will receive guidance that will enable you to gain a more comprehensive comprehension of the methods by which you shall address a given circumstance. You will enhance your ability to effectively address negativity or challenging situations due to the presence of a supportive individual who will guide you through the coping process, which proves to be immensely potent and advantageous.

Cognitive Restructuring

Cognitive restructuring is a widely employed procedure in various therapeutic modalities, particularly those incorporating cognitive-based approaches. It demonstrates a remarkable efficacy, necessitating an understanding and appreciation of the inherent influence it imparts within the domain of competition. The ability to reorganize and reshape one's thoughts is a profoundly effective method for self-improvement. Simply put, acquiring the skill to initiate and maintain command over one's thoughts is the sole task at hand.

Positivity

Indeed, positivity has the inherent ability to counterbalance and nullify the negativity ingrained within your thoughts. It can be employed on a regular basis in order to ascertain the necessary knowledge, cognitive processes, and strategic methods for tackling challenging circumstances. Once you acquire the knowledge of effectively cultivating positive thinking, you will acquire the ability to swiftly and effortlessly alter your mindset. Simply replacing negativity with positivity will naturally lead to the desired outcome.

Mindfulness

Mindfulness entails the skill of halting one's thoughts and residing fully in the current moment. Through pausing and mindfully observing one's surroundings, one can typically discern their emotional state with great accuracy. Once you have ascertained your emotional state, you can then proceed to analyze the underlying cognitive processes contributing to your current disposition. Subsequently, you will be equipped to effectively determine the most appropriate course of action for engaging with the individual you are interacting with. Consider the following: if one were to experience feelings of anger, it would be possible to engage in a conscientious process of self-awareness, acknowledging and accepting that anger is present, and subsequently utilizing this awareness to prevent oneself from expressing anger in an impulsive or aggressive manner.

Gratitude

An additional prevalent technique that can serve as a dependable source of enhancing one's positive mindset is expressing gratitude. Once you are able to pause and acknowledge your existing possessions, you can then prompt yourself to refrain from relinquishing them. One can engage in the practice of reminding oneself that a situation may possess both negative and positive aspects. One possibility is that you possess a devoted and loyal confidante, or that you perceive yourself as exceptionally fortuitous to be experiencing the current bond you share. In the event of a disagreement, it is possible to take solace in the presence of lingering positivity, thereby tempering the negative aspects of the situation. The practice of expressing gratitude effectively eradicates negative emotions associated with unfulfilled desires and the perception of falling short of expectations. Having a sense of gratitude indicates that there is still something worthwhile to strive for, as it naturally inclines you towards embracing positivity. Similar to the aforementioned methods, this particular approach also holds potential for integrating positive outcomes that will prove advantageous to both yourself and your immediate surroundings.

Step 2: Recognize Your Value

Were you aware that individuals who possess unwavering self-assurance often exhibit a strong inclination for making decisive choices? An aspect that is quite commendable in accomplished individuals is their ability to swiftly arrive at decisions of lesser significance without undue delay. They do not engage in excessive analysis. One of the contributing factors to their ability to make prompt decisions is their comprehensive understanding of the overarching vision and ultimate objective.

However, would it be possible for you to articulate your desired definition?

The initial step is to establish and articulate your core principles. As per the opinion shared by acclaimed author

Tony Robbins, there exist two primary categories of values, namely end values and means values. These two categories of values are interconnected with the desired emotional state, encompassing happiness, a feeling of security, and overall satisfaction, to name a few.

Means Values

These are mere means by which one can elicit the desired emotion. An exemplary illustration can be found in the concept of money, which frequently functions as a means rather than an ultimate objective. It represents an avenue towards achieving financial independence, a desirable outcome that you aspire for and therefore holds inherent significance.

Ends Values

This pertains to the various emotional states one seeks, such as affection, contentment, and a feeling of being protected. They represent the offerings of your financial resources. For example, the funds will provide you with assurance and economic security.

Put simply, the means value pertains to the things that individuals perceive as desirable, and are pursued in order to ultimately achieve the end values. It is of utmost significance that you possess a clear understanding of your core values, in order to facilitate the making of well-informed decisions with enhanced efficiency. Consequently, this will instill within you a profound sense of self and serve as the everlasting wellspring of your confidence. It is imperative to maintain control over one's life rather than allowing it to dictate one's actions.

One approach to achieve this is by ensuring the clear definition of your desired final outcomes. You can initiate the process by allocating a minimum of one to two hours per week to diligently record your ultimate core principles. To reach your destination, commence by explicitly articulating the core principles you intend to develop in order to actualize your ideal existence.

Here are several inquiries that could aid in gaining a comprehensive understanding of the situation:

What are the most significant aspects of your life?

Are there aspects in your life that you hold little concern for?

In the event of facing a challenging decision, which guiding principles would you adhere to, and which ones would you choose to disregard?

If you are a parent or have children, what are some of the principles you would imbue in them?

Step 3: Cultivate personal contentment

Contentment is a decision that one can make, and the most formidable barriers often arise from self-imposed limitations, such as believing oneself undeserving of joy.

If you do not perceive yourself as deserving of joy, then you are also lacking belief in your entitlement to the positive aspects of life, the components that bring you happiness, ultimately impeding your ability to experience true happiness.

You can be happier. It relies on your choice of what you direct your attention towards. Thus, choose happiness.

Happiness is not an occurrence that befalls upon you. It is a matter of personal agency, yet it necessitates exertion. Do not rely on external sources to derive happiness, as this could lead to an interminable wait. No external individual or factor possesses the ability to bestow upon you a state of happiness.

Joy is an inherent sentiment that originates from within oneself. Only 10 percent of your happiness can be attributed to external factors. The remaining 90% pertains to one's conduct and the mindset embraced when confronted with such circumstances. The empirical formula for happiness consists of external circumstances accounting for 10%, genetic predisposition contributing 50%, and deliberate actions - encompassing learning and exercises - constituting the remaining 40%. Certain individuals possess an innate predisposition towards greater happiness, whereas those who are inherently less happy can cultivate their happiness through engaging in the suggested exercises, surpassing even those individuals who were initially more joyful but do not partake in such practices. Both equations share the commonality that external circumstances have a minimal impact on our overall happiness.

It is customary for us to presume that our circumstances possess a considerably larger influence on our overall well-being. An intriguing aspect lies in the notion that happiness frequently manifests itself when one ceases their relentless pursuit of it. Take pleasure in every single moment. Anticipate the occurrence of extraordinary events and advantageous circumstances at every turn, and eventually you will encounter them. Irrespective of your subject of attention, an increased perception of it might be observed. Select to prioritize opportunities, ascertain to direct attention towards the positive aspects, and opt to center attention on attaining happiness. Make your own happiness.

www.ingramcontent.com/pod-product-compliance
Lightning Source LLC
Chambersburg PA
CBHW052146110526
44591CB00012B/1874